Published by Creative Education
123 South Broad Street, Mankato, Minnesota 56001
Creative Education is an imprint of The Creative Company

Art direction by Rita Marshall
Production design by The Design Lab

Photographs by Corbis (W. Perry Conway, Yann Arthus-Bertrand), Fred Hood,
The Image Finders (Jim Baron, Kent Foster, Werner Lobert), Alison M. Jones,
Tom Myers, John Perryman, Root Resources (Stan Osolinski, W. Anderson/Visual Echoes),
James P. Rowan, Kevin Schafer, Tom Stack & Associates (Erwin & Peggy Bauer,
Joe McDonald, John Gerlach), Ted Whiting

Library of Congress Cataloging-in-Publication Data

Kalz, Jill.
Cheetahs / by Jill Kalz.
p. cm. — (Let's investigate)
Summary: Describes the physical characteristics, behavior, and natural
environment of this endangered creature, the fastest land animal on Earth.
ISBN 1-58341-232-8
1. Cheetah—Juvenile literature. [1. Cheetah.
2. Endangered species.] I. Title. II. Series.
QL737.C23 K355   2002
599.75'9—dc21   2001047894

First edition

2   4   6   8   9   7   5   3   1

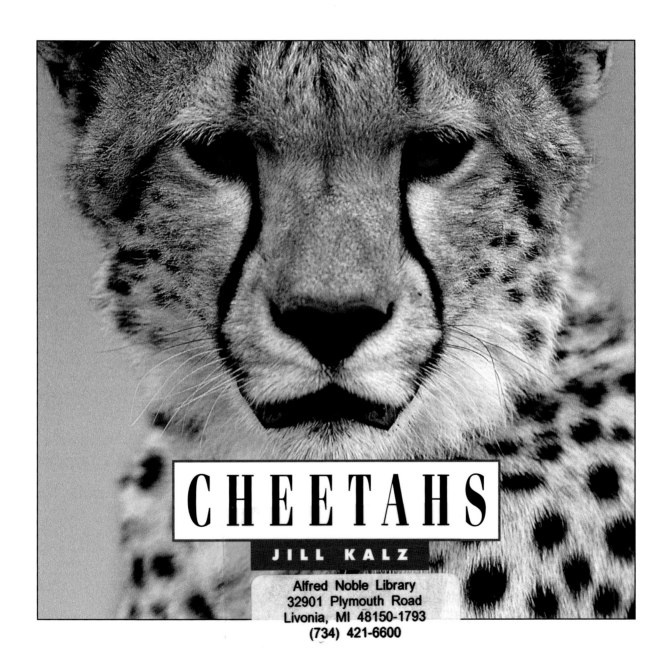

CHEETAHS

JILL KALZ

Creative Education

CHEETAH
FAMILY

All cats, including cheetahs, lions, leopards, and house cats, belong to the Felidae *family. Members of this family are called felids (FEE-ledz).*

Above, a male lion
Right, a cheetah in full sprint

Millions of years ago, long before lions and leopards existed, cheetahs ruled the world's open plains with their speed. They sprinted across the prairies of Europe, Asia, North America, and Africa. Throughout history, cheetahs have been worshipped, trained for sport, and kept as symbols of wealth and power. But today, these elegant cats are in a race for survival.

CHEETAH
IDENTITY

At first glance, leopards may look like cheetahs, but they are much heavier and covered with rosette-shaped spots, not round ones. Leopards also lack "tear marks."

**Right, an adult cheetah
Below, a cheetah's distinctive "tear marks"**

SPEED AND GRACE

Compared to some of its relatives, the cheetah (*Acinonyx jubatus*) is a rather small cat. An adult cheetah can weigh up to 140 pounds (64 kg) and measure four feet (1.2 m) from end to end. A grown lion, by comparison, weighs an average of 500 pounds (227 kg) and may be nine feet (2.7 m) long.

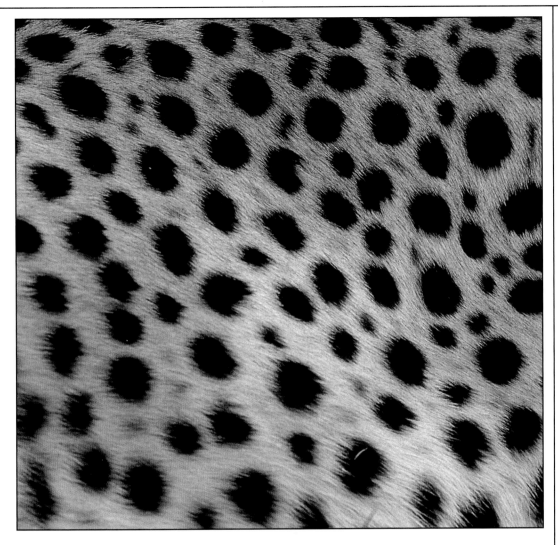

CHEETAH
FASHION

During the early 1970s, hundreds of cheetahs were killed each month so their skins could be made into fur coats.

The cheetah is covered with coarse, golden-tan fur and round, black spots. Long, black lines called "tear marks" run from the inner corners of its eyes to its mouth. The cheetah's belly is white, as is the tip of its black-ringed tail. It's difficult to tell male and female cheetahs apart, but males are usually a bit bigger.

A cheetah's fur pattern blends easily into tall, dry grasses

CHEETAH

ORIGIN

Based on fossil findings, **paleontologists** *believe cheetahs originated in North America in what is now Nevada, Texas, and Wyoming.*

CHEETAH

STRIDE

At full speed, a cheetah can cover 26 feet (8 m) in a single stride and complete three or four strides in one second.

A sprinting cheetah in mid-stride

Every part of a cheetah's lean body is designed for speed, from its long, muscular legs to its strong heart and large lungs. Its flexible spine acts like a spring. When a cheetah runs, its spine arches and all four feet are pulled together. When its spine uncoils, the cheetah's feet are thrust out, and the cat appears to fly. The cheetah can reach a speed of 45 miles (72 km) per hour in just two seconds, quickly topping out at an astonishing 70 miles (113 km) per hour. This makes cheetahs the fastest land animals on

Earth. But cheetahs are sprinters, not long-distance runners. They usually can't sustain their top speed for more than a minute.

Cheetahs have **non-retractable** claws. Short and blunt, the claws provide cheetahs with little defense against enemies but provide excellent traction during chases, gripping the ground like cleats on a track runner's shoe. A 30-inch (76 cm) tail helps to balance the cat so it doesn't spin out during quick, tight turns.

CHEETAH
CLAWS

*Although most of its claws are dull, the cheetah has one sharp, curved claw, called a dewclaw, high up on the inside of each wrist. The cat uses it to knock **prey** off balance during a chase.*

CHEETAH

CLIMBING

Unlike leopards, cheetahs aren't tree-dwelling cats, although they may climb a tree to scout prey or leave territorial scent marks.

CHEETAH

AGE

Cheetahs in the wild usually live about five to seven years. In captivity, they may live 12 to 15 years.

Acacia trees dot the sparse African savanna

WIDE, OPEN SPACES

Today, more than 12,000 wild cheetahs make their home in Africa. An additional 200 live in Asia, in Iran. Cheetahs thrive in large, open spaces, and the **savannas** of eastern and southern Africa are ideal. There, cheetahs have clear views of approaching herds, tall grasses to hide amongst, and plenty of room to chase down prey.

CHEETAH
THIRST

Cheetahs can go 5 to 10 days without water, surviving on the water contained in the meat they eat.

During Africa's rainy season, the plains are carpeted with lush **vegetation**, and **herbivores**, such as antelope and wildebeest, are plentiful and provide food for cheetahs. But during the dry season, water holes shrink and the plains turn brown. The herds of herbivores **migrate** in search of water and green plants. Female cheetahs usually follow the herds, covering as many as 300 square miles (777 sq km). Most males stay within their territories. These areas usually cover about 12 square miles (31 sq km). Males mark their territories by spraying bushes and trees with urine. Any male who wanders into another male's territory is attacked. Females are ignored unless they are ready to mate.

Above, a cheetah taking a drink
Left, a migrating herd of wildebeest

CHEETAH
MEALS

When antelope or antelope-like prey is scarce, cheetahs will also eat young ostriches, rabbits, frogs, lizards, warthogs, zebras, and fruit such as the juicy tsama melon.

Above, a guinea fowl, potential cheetah prey Right, a cheetah atop a termite mound

FEEDING HABITS

Cheetahs are diurnal, which means they are active during the day and rest at night. They prefer to hunt in the early mornings and late afternoons, out of the hot sun. They rely on their eyesight to hunt and can spot prey up to three miles (4.8 km) away. Termite mounds make excellent lookout posts. In East Africa, some mounds may be up to 30 feet (9 m) tall!

Human teeth are flat, wide, and designed for grinding. They work like pliers. Cheetah teeth are narrow and sharp and work like scissors.

13

Cheetahs are **carnivores**. Although they will eat small prey such as rabbits and game birds, they prefer hoofed animals such as antelope and impalas. Thomson's gazelles, or Tommies, are the cheetah's favorite prey.

Above, a cheetah's scissor-like teeth Left, a Thomson's gazelle on alert

CHEETAH

SECONDS

Tigers often return to their kills for second helpings, and leopards store their kills in trees. But cheetahs simply eat their fill and then walk away, leaving the rest to scavengers.

Right, a camouflaged cheetah
Far right, a cheetah stalking prey

nce a cheetah has set its sights on an animal, it creeps through the tall grass, body low to the ground, **camouflaged** by its gold and black-spotted coat.

When the cheetah is within 50 yards (46 m) of its victim, it explodes from cover with a burst of speed. The surprised animal bolts, but it's usually no match for the cheetah. The chase often lasts less than 20 seconds and ends when

CHEETAH
DINNER

Cheetahs eat only fresh meat and rarely eat an animal they haven't killed themselves. This makes it extremely difficult to trap them with bait.

the cheetah swipes the animal's rump with its front paw, knocking the animal off balance. The animal stumbles to the ground, and the cheetah quickly clamps its jaws around the animal's windpipe to suffocate it.

Young cheetahs with a freshly killed gazelle

CHEETAH
F O O D

Thomson's gazelles, the cheetah's favorite prey animals, are small antelope that stand about 28 inches (71 cm) tall. Each has about 15 pounds (6.8 kg) of meat on it.

The chase requires a tremendous amount of energy, and a cheetah may rest up to 30 minutes afterward, panting like a dog. When it does eat, it gulps its food down quickly. Because the cheetah is built for speed, not fighting, it can't defend its kills from larger **predators**. Lions, hyenas, and even flocks of vultures will often steal the cheetah's kill, and the cheetah can do nothing but watch.

A cheetah resting in the shade after feeding

MOTHERS AND CUBS

Cheetahs mate year-round. Female cheetahs first mate when they are about two years old. Males usually wait a bit longer. When a female cheetah is ready to mate, her urine takes on a special scent. The **dominant** male in the area follows this scent to the female and the two spend up to a week together. If the female becomes pregnant, she will give birth to cubs three months later. After mating, the male leaves, and the female is on her own.

CHEETAH
GENDER

People often have specific names for male and female animals, such as buck and doe, cock and hen, stallion and mare. All cheetahs, however, are simply called "cheetah."

CHEETAH
COURTSHIP

During the mating period, a male and female cheetah playfully chase each other, tumble on the ground, and make chirping sounds like birds.

The courtship period between male and female cheetahs is brief

CHEETAH
HANDLES

All cats, including cheetahs, carry their young the same way: by the nape of the neck. Loose folds of skin serve as natural handles.

CHEETAH
OUTINGS

Cheetah cubs use the white tip of their mother's tail as a guide when following her through tall grasses. They almost always follow single-file.

A female cheetah watching over her cubs

C heetah litters may contain up to eight cubs, although three or four is average. Blind and weighing just 9 to 15 ounces (255–425 g), newborn cubs are helpless and totally dependent on their mother. But they grow quickly. Within 5 to 10 days, their eyes open and they begin to crawl.

At two weeks, tiny teeth appear, and at three weeks, the cubs are walking. Their mother continues to nurse them for six to eight weeks. After that time, cubs share in their mother's kill.

Until they are about three months old, cheetah cubs are covered with fluffy, smoke-gray fur. Longer, thicker fur, called a mantle, grows along their back, neck, and head. The dark coat helps cubs hide in the shadows, and the mantle sometimes fools predators, such as lions and hyenas, into thinking that the cubs are ratels—small, vicious, skunk-colored animals that most predators avoid.

CHEETAH
ORPHANS

Most cheetah cubs die if their mother is killed, but some are adopted, usually by mothers with cubs of their own. Small groups of males will sometimes adopt orphaned cubs too.

Above, a cub with a well-defined mantle

CHEETAH
TRAINING

When cubs pounce, hide, wrestle, and nip at their siblings during play, they're actually developing their hunting skills. Their mother often plays with them too.

CHEETAH
FORMATION

When a cheetah mother shares a kill with her cubs, each cat approaches it from a different side so that, from above, they form a star shape around the dead animal.

Growing cheetah cubs sharing a kill provided by their mother

For the first six weeks, cubs stay hidden while their mother goes out and hunts. Young cubs are easy prey for predators, so to protect them, the female cheetah moves them every few days to a new hiding spot. Unfortunately, despite her efforts and her cubs' natural camouflage, nearly 90 percent of all cheetah cubs die during this time due to predator attacks.

CHEETAH
COMMUNICATION

Cheetahs are best known for their bird-like chirps and loud purring, but they also yelp, hiss, growl, bleat, and bark. One sound they can't make, however, is a roar.

Above, a hissing cheetah
Right, a coalition of young cheetahs

When a female cheetah's cubs are 12 to 18 months old, she abandons them to mate again and start a new family. By this time, the cubs have lost their mantles, grown adult coats, and learned how to hunt. Female cubs soon go their separate ways to find mates, but brothers may remain lifelong companions, forming groups called coalitions.

ROYAL HUNTERS

People have long admired the cheetah for its hunting abilities and elegance. Ancient Egyptians considered cheetahs sacred. Their goddess Mafdet took the form of a cheetah. In 3000 B.C., the Sumerians, people who lived in what is now Iraq, first tamed cheetahs and kept them as pets.

CHEETAH
ROYALTY

Even though it has a special name, the king cheetah, a cheetah covered in black blotches, is not a separate sub-species but an African cheetah with a rare fur mutation.

23

Above and left, rare king cheetahs

CHEETAH
SPOTS

A cheetah's spot pattern is like a human's fingerprint. No two cheetahs have the same arrangement of spots.

As early as the fifth century A.D., nobles in Europe and Asia kept cheetahs as symbols of wealth and used them for sport. During the 15th and 16th centuries, Italian noblemen brought cheetahs along with them when they went out to hunt rabbits and deer. Akbar the Great, an Indian emperor, reportedly kept 9,000 cheetahs and used many of them for a sport called "coursing." In this sport, a cheetah was blindfolded and taken into an open field. When the blindfold was removed, the cheetah sprinted across the field toward its target, usually a gazelle. An audience cheered as the cheetah ran down its prey.

Even hares aren't quick enough to outrun the agile cheetah

Running from Extinction

Cheetahs and pumas, or cougars, evolved about five and a half million years ago. By contrast, lions and tigers evolved just one and a half million years ago.

25

SURVIVAL STRUGGLE

Today, the cheetah is classified as an endangered species. This means that if nothing is done to save it, the cheetah could soon become **extinct**. Since 1900, the number of cheetahs has decreased from 100,000 to 12,000, and that number continues to fall.

*Above, a tiger
Left, a poster drawing attention to the cheetah's struggle*

CHEETAH
REFUGE

The Serengeti National Park, home to a number of cheetahs, is located in Tanzania, East Africa. It is about the size of Connecticut.

Part of the African wilderness, now parceled out as farmland

One reason for the cheetah's decline is the loss of **habitat**. As human populations in parts of Africa increase, more land is fenced off for farmland and livestock pastures. Wild grazing animals are forced to migrate to more wooded areas, but cheetahs can't follow since they need wide, open spaces to hunt. The cheetahs must compete with other predators on the shrinking savanna for limited food supplies. In order to survive, cheetahs sometimes resort to killing cattle. Sadly,

many cheetahs are then shot because of this.

Poachers are another cheetah threat. Despite laws that make killing cheetahs illegal (except when they threaten livestock or people), many people continue to sell cheetah skins. As the cheetah population declines, the skins become more valuable, and so poachers kill even more cheetahs.

CHEETAH
PROTECTION

In addition to using guard dogs, some African ranchers use guard donkeys to scare cheetahs away from their livestock.

CHEETAH
SOCIETY

Cheetahs are both solitary and social animals. Females live alone, except when they have a litter. Males prefer to live in groups of two or three.

CHEETAH

BREEDING

Akbar the Great was unable to breed more than one cheetah litter in captivity. The next captive birth didn't occur until 1956—more than 400 years later—in Philadelphia, Pennsylvania.

A cheetah in captivity

Cheetahs are very difficult to breed in captivity. More than half of all zoos that have tried have failed. The main reason for this is that cheetahs lack variation in their **genes**. Four species of cheetahs once roamed the earth. Ten thousand years ago, three species and most of the fourth died out. That left just a small group of closely related cheetahs to breed with one another. As a result, each cheetah today shares 99 percent of its genes with every other cheetah. (By contrast, humans share just 68 percent with

one another.) It's almost like each cheetah is an identical twin. Without enough gene variation, animals cannot adapt to change or resist disease. If one cheetah falls victim to a fatal disease, all other cheetahs will likely die from it too.

CHEETAH
CAPITAL

Namibia, a country in southern Africa, is the unofficial cheetah capital of the world. About 2,500 wild cheetahs live there.

T hankfully, there are organizations that are working to save the cheetah. One of these is the Cheetah Conservation Fund (CCF) in Namibia. CCF works with ranchers to find ways to live peacefully with cheetahs and educates them on non-lethal protection methods such as guard dogs and live capture. Zoo breeding programs help, but the long-term survival of the cheetah truly depends upon the health and success of free-ranging cheetahs in Africa and Asia.

Free-ranging cheetahs on the Serengeti Plains of Africa

C heetahs are the gentlest wild cats in the world. When faced with danger, they flee rather than fight. So it's up to us to fight for them in their battle for survival. By supporting the efforts of organizations such as the CCF and encouraging countries to make chee-tah protection a priority, we can help make sure that the fastest land animal on Earth wins the race against extinction.

CHEETAH
AMBASSADORS

In April 2001, the Namibian govern-ment donated 10 cheetahs to the United States. North American zoos are currently home to about 250 cheetahs.

Glossary

A **camouflaged** animal blends in with its surroundings so it can't be seen.

Animals that eat meat as the main part of their diet are called **carnivores**.

A **dominant** male or female is superior to all other males or females, either because of its age, size, or strength.

An animal that is **extinct** no longer exists anywhere on Earth.

Genes are tiny units in cells that offspring inherit from their parents. Genes define all of the offspring's features, such as size, coloring, and personality.

The place where an animal normally lives is called its **habitat**.

Herbivores are animals that eat plants as the main part of their diet.

When animals **migrate**, they travel from one region or climate to another, often to feed or breed.

If claws are **non-retractable**, they cannot be pulled back into the paws.

Paleontologists are scientists who study prehistoric plant and animal remains.

Poachers are people who steal or kill wild animals illegally, usually to make money.

Animals that hunt and kill other animals for food are called **predators**. The animals they hunt are called **prey**.

Savannas are flat, grassy areas with few trees located in hot, dry climates.

The array of plant life in an area is called **vegetation**.

Index